a very special thank you and dedication to

California Farm Families

J.L.D.

To the memory of my father, Ken Jones, his small orchard and to his children and grandchildren with whom he lovingly shared the fruit: Rocky, Jenith, Craig, Paul, Heath, Maayan, Shaki, Shannon, Joe, Brandon, Andrea, Brittany, Hannah, and Taylor.

R.M.G.

To my kids: Julia, Justin and Lauren, who grew up playing in irrigation ditches.

ORCHARDS IN THE VALLEY

a California Tale

Written by Janice L. Dodson

Illustrated by Rosemary Manly Gamblin

Dodson, Janice. Orchards in the Valley, A California Tale
Summary: a valley is settled, orchards planted, produce enjoyed, but more people arrive, orchards chopped down to build, yet some survive.

[1. Orchards-Fiction. 2. Agriculture-Fiction. 3. Produce-Fiction.   4. Fruit-Fiction.
5. Cherries-Fiction. 6. California history-Fiction. 7. Development-Fiction.
8. Stories in Rhyme.]

ISBN: 978-1-945526-43-5

Library of Congress Catalog Number: 2018945811

Once there was a valley
a golden place to be.

To the west hills rose
then tumbled down to the sea.

To the east rolling hills
with oak trees scattered through
soared into mountains
where giant sequoias grew.

In the majestic mountains
rain came down as snow,

melted in the springtime
and made the rivers flow

down the rolling hills
and through the valley below.

The soil was dark and rich
perfect for orchards to grow
one of the best places on earth
to till, plant, and sow.

Settlers came to the valley
and planted fruit and nut trees.

They used water from the rivers;
pollination from bees.

Long days of their hard toil
and the sun's bright light and heat
grew orchards of cherries
and other good food to eat.

Year after year
crops were picked.

Stands dotted country roads
where the fresh produce was sold.

But most was packed in sheds
with care

then trucked
to city grocery stores

or sent to the East by train

or shipped to far-off shores:
cherries to Japan,
walnuts to Spain.

More people came.
Communities were planned

throughout the valley
and needed more land.

Orchards stood in the way.
Many would not be saved
from buildings to be built
and new roads to be paved.

Many trees were chopped down
and orchards went away.

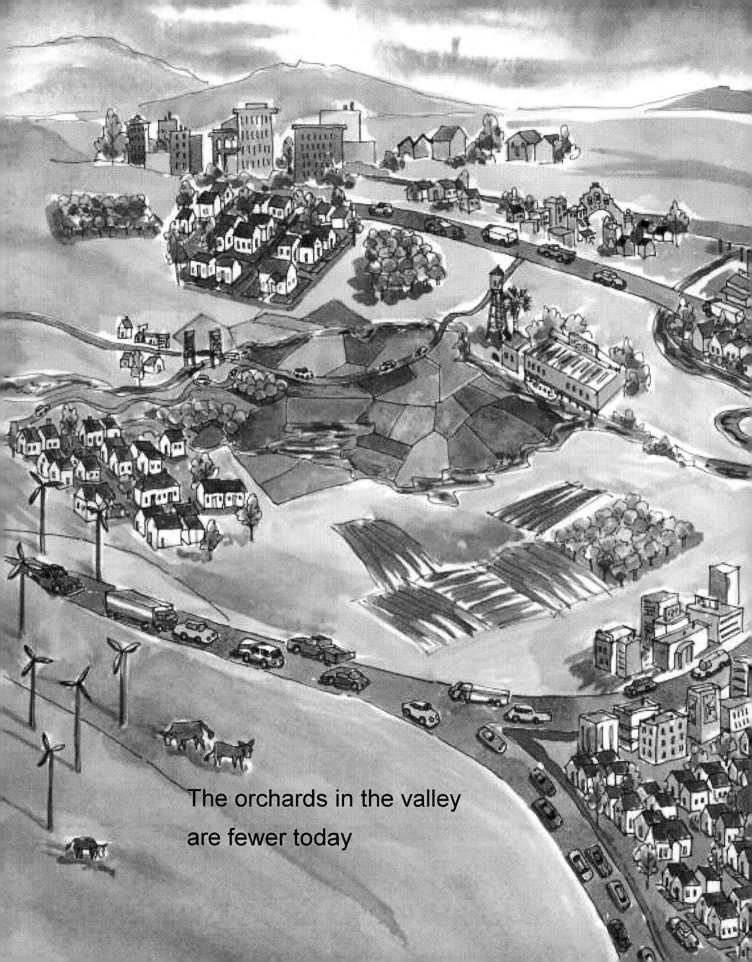

The orchards in the valley
are fewer today

producing less good food to eat
and life in the valley is not as sweet.

Thankfully, there are
still people who know
that we must leave room
for cherries to grow.

For that we can be grateful
each time that we eat

. . . produce from

valley orchards . . .

. . . and cherries so sweet.